To Heather

WITH
Compliments.

READ IT AND WEEP
(AND YOU WILL!)
I'VE HAD FUN!!

Gordon

I asked myself a few searching questions
before carrying on with this.

1) Isn't it a little arrogant and
   presumptuous for an "unknown" to
   write not one, but two
   autobiographies?
   Possibly. But why shouldn't an
   unknown tell his or her story. Maybe I
   will become less unknown. I love
   reading about other people, famous or
   otherwise.
2) Would anyone be interested enough
   to buy it?
   The world is full of curious people.
   Ordinary, or seemingly ordinary
   people can be just as interesting as
   those who live in the bright lights.

3) Isn't a sign of an inflated ego? A bit pretentious and delusional?

Well – I wouldn't mind a little bit of ego inflation; just a slight lift mind.

And, I love pretending. I am not aware of any mistaken belief; this is not a figment of my imagination.

First off - I had no intention whatsoever of publishing this brief excursion.

So why have I?

Because, a seed was sown and it took root. Some good soul having read my little autobiography – "You Don't Have To Be Mad", asked if there was more – the fool! Of course there was but I'd never considered carrying on in that vein because I was focusing on the 'proper book', as I call it. Then, I realized that I'd already written most of it. I just needed to dig it out and do a little editing; well, quite a bit of editing to be honest.

I went right over it and thought: "Yes – this has mileage". And it was great fun revisiting it.

Specifically – it covers a few years when I took a career break from nursing and decided to explore other worlds. I did it because I could and circumstances permitted. I still needed a job but the pressure was off.

As it turned out, it was quite a journey. I was turning my hand to something different.

Then – I broke a leg . . . . !

Knickers?

What about knickers?

Well – I was working on behalf of a leading, high profile High Street retailer, which has a reputation for quality ladies lingerie, and the job was all about getting these products, and others, from the warehouse on to the shop floor.

The company which managed the facility acted as a sub-contractor overseeing the distribution of the goods right around the country.

The type of goods in the warehouse was quite comprehensive and wide-ranging, as befits a major High Street retailer; but the most prolific was, without doubt, knickers and bras! All shapes and all sizes and – all too frequently – the butt of endless amusement. No pun intended.

One's day was spent going up and down narrow aisles picking items off the shelves ready to send off to the stores around the country. It was undemanding and fairly easy going. You had to concentrate and make sure the right item had been picked as there were so many similarities, but it wasn't over-taxing. In fact, it could get a little boring.

The thing is, these shelves were up to 40 feet high. If you suffered from vertigo or acrophobia, you were screwed.

To access the items, you made use of a twin-beamed order picker; a foul beast of a machine invented by the devil himself. (Why is the devil a "he"?) Anyway – I hated these awkward and cumbersome things and never truly mastered them.

There is a picture of a similar one at the end of the story.

The aisles were quite narrow, as well as high. The platform picker we used was not as wide as the one in the picture, but it was about the same length.

There were quite a few aisles – about 20, as I recall; however the number of pickers was barely half of that. This meant that they had to be manoeuvred out, and very carefully and gently, into the required aisle.

There was just enough room to accommodate the length of the machine which made turning extremely challenging. It took real skill, a skill which eluded me. I was forever crashing it into the shelving racks causing them to shake perilously and those working either side in other aisles to bombard me with abuse as they feared for their lives.

The potential for serious damage was considerable. In the end I was effectively banned from using them; the company weren't sure their insurance would cover it! As a result, I was assigned to the stultifying job of preparing and checking orders.

I hated this as well!!! I wasn't doing very well, was I?

The picking bit was quite straightforward for the most part; however, ladies lingerie was a bit of a minefield. I was staggered at the range of shapes, sizes and styles. There was no such a thing as a "simple" pair of knickers, and bras, well, they were a real mind-bender.

The choices on offer were Thongs, "Gs", High Leg, Low Leg, Bikini, Midi, Brazilian and "Full Support". Wow! How does one choose?

A bloke just has to decide on whether or not to have a "Willy Hole"; or, I suppose – it's Boxers or Briefs?

And there was no such thing as a humble brassiere.

First Bras, Padded Bras, Wired and Non-Wired, Plunge, Push-Up, Sports, Strapless, Full Cup, Half Cup, Tea Cup(!) – bloody hell, it's mind-boggling!!

Then, the poor woman has to get the right "cup". A, AA, C, D, DD, E, F, FF? It goes on and on!

Women have always impressed me with their fortitude, tolerance and stoicism, but I never realized that buying underwear required a degree in physics!

Bach's "Air On A G String" took on a whole new meaning.

Anyway – "the job".

It was never meant to be anything long term, but I'd hoped for something more in the way of job satisfaction. After that bumpy, (and I do mean bumpy), start, I managed to wangle myself a cushy number in the warehouse office doing relatively simple but important clerical work. Sending up order sheets, filing completed orders and verifying stock balance. The two people I worked with were great company and very easy to work with. The work environment was bright, cheery and relatively peaceful. I felt that I'd found my niche.

I was also given an occasional escape, just to add a bit of variety.

One of the supervisors suggested I might like to train on the fork-lift, which was used to move ground level stock stored on racks 10 feet high, spaced around the sides of the warehouse.

I soon got the hang of it and was spinning, (quite literally), around like a real pro! I'd be called out of the office for a while to shift a bit of stock then return to my desk.

Oh – I haven't mentioned the bright red two-piece uniforms; bloody awful. We all looked like escapees from a Father Christmas convention.

Also – security is well worth a mention. Because of the "vulnerability" of the stock, we all had to endure occasional searches. The "feel and fondle", as it became know. It could have been all too easy to filch a few pairs knickers deftly removed from their packaging. Indeed, I understand that someone tried to walk out *wearing* 12 pairs of size 16 Lycra Briefs; although I'm not sure if the slippery thief was male or female. Anyway – they weren't slippery enough as the bulge created by the multi-layered knickers was noticed by a slick pair of fondling digits.

This was a real eye-opener and an interesting experience. It was a world away from my career path.

If nothing else, it was certainly different.

Yes, it could get a bit boring and tedious and my mind, hungry for a little bit more in the way of stimulation, would occasionally wander. That's when I got my double A mixed up with my double D.

I will never forget those awful red uniforms and those accursed platform pickers, I wasn't too sure about the fondling, possibly because the 'fondler' was built like a brick privy and had a face like an deformed Ugli Fruit. I'm sorry, I'm no oil painting; (well maybe a Jackson Pollack), but this guy could turn you to stone. It was like being groped by a JCB.

Never-the-less; it can be said that my work

experience was greatly enhanced by knickers!

I'm usually loathe to say much about my colleagues but here I will make an exception. There were 5 supervisors. Three ladies and two men. The ladies were really lovely; so supportive and encouraging. Likewise, one of the guys was an affable and pleasant bloke, who would agree to anything just for a quiet life. The other chap, however, was one of the most racist, misogynistic, arrogant buggers I have ever worked with. A real shit! He seemed to enjoy being unpopular and delighted in irritating others. I had never worked with such an arrogant bastard before and I'd been around. I just could not fathom the guy.

I write this in 2018, when I am quite sure he wouldn't last five minutes. For some obscure and inexplicable reason – he was tolerated.

Even though – he was intolerable!

I wasn't unhappy here, but never settled. It was fun in the office and I enjoyed the wheel spins on the fork lift but nothing really clicked.

Now what . . . . ?

The "Picker"

Bit Of A Stink

This little venture wasn't as outside the box as it might seem. I saw an opportunity to utilize some of my latent engineering skills, although I'm not sure latent is the right word. After 20 odd years, they were positively moribund.

I accepted this 12 week post because the base site was a mere 15/20 minute walk from home. However, the sewage plants I'd be visiting were some 8/10 miles away located deep within the countryside. Perhaps it was the policy to hide them away out in the hinterlands?

The temporary position was to cover for a guy called Jeff who'd was on extended sick-leave following a major operation.

My guide and mentor for the duration, was a person, who, for me, epitomized the term (or expression) – "a real character"; a larger than life individual called Pete.

I often struggle to describe him because I tend to end up sounding snobbish and denigrating, which is unjust and misleading. Pete was a kind and fair man. He came across as hard and surly but that was just a crust to a distinctly soft centre; not that he was a "softy".

A ruddy, corpulent bloke, he'd have benefitted from losing a few stone, but it somehow enhanced his jovial and ebullient nature.

Now this is where it might seem a wee bit snobby or high-brow. Pete was not one for decorum. He was a base and fundamental guy who cared little or nothing for airs and graces; and he swore like a sapper. No, he swore like and army of sappers. He'd belch, fart and curse regardless of who was around. Prince or Pauper, everyone was equal in his eyes. He made it crystal clear that he had no time for the nobility or the privileged few.

"Bunch of fucking wasters," he'd growl angrily. "Load of fucking parasites, the lot of 'em."

See what I mean about language? And he also used the "C" word with alacrity and relish.

Now – before I hear cries of "Hypocrite!"; yes, I'm no saint and such profanities sometimes roll off my tongue. I can go 24 hours without swearing, if I concentrate really hard. It was the sheer intensity of bad language which made Pete so prolific.

Along with Pete and myself, there were two other guys: Keith and Ron; each 'team' looked after 3 sewage plants each.

I immediately got the impression that the 'other team' were not that keen on Pete. They appeared to be – shall I say; smarter guys. In fact, I'm sure they felt sorry for me. Whatever – for better or worse, I was at the 'mercy' of Pete for the next few weeks.

First day – I turned up to find Pete, Keith and Ron in the base office arguing with the area manager – Mr Paget. That is – Pete was arguing with him; most aggressively. Keith and Ron were trying to be more conciliatory. The first thing I heard as I walked in to the room was – "Fucking bullshit!".

Oh boy!

"Typical fucking management babble. Like those silly bastards know what they're talking about!"

Eventually, the discussion reached a conclusion and we hit the road, heading out to one of 'our' sewage plants. Pete continued to grumble about matters, which didn't really concern or interest me. I was just passing through, after all.

He was not a happy man and grunted, belched and farted all the way. The 8 miles or so to our first port of call seemed like a 100.

On arrival, we went into the little office come workshop, then Pete took me on a brief tour of the plant outlining what needed to be done. It all seemed fairly straightforward and there didn't appear to be anything too daunting. Pete then gave me a few simple jobs to get on with before retiring to the office. This suited me, I was more than happy to get on with things – and be left alone. As you will have gathered by now; Pete was a very overpowering and overwhelming presence.

I spent a contented few hours clearing runnels, filters and topping up oil wells on the water pumps. It wasn't exactly rocket science requiring fundamental common sense as much as any particular knowledge. I was quite surprised at some of the things which collected in and around the filters; not in the least, money! Yes – a fair amount of coinage settles into the outlet channels. Largely small value coins, but there were quite a few fifty pence pieces and pound coins. And – because they'd been through the filters, they were fairly 'clean'. No filthy lucre here.

I also fished out an exotic looking basque, as in ladies' underwear. It seemed to be in be in remarkably good condition and I marvelled that it had got this far. One wondered how the hell it ended up there in the first place?

The real bugbear and the cause of considerable problems were ladies sanitary products and disposable nappies. Oh – and flipping condoms!

I took the money back to the office to show Pete, I didn't bother with the basque.

I found him sitting, head back, mouth agape, snoring. It made me feel a bit queasy because he still had half a corned beef sandwich in his mouth.

I pondered the wisdom of waking him up as I was quite enjoying my own company. Sadly – he woke up and tried desperately, (and pointlessly), to pretend that he hadn't been asleep.

"Ah. Right. Just catching up on some paperwork. How's it going, then? Nothing to worry about?"

There was nothing to worry about apart from the fact that it was nearly time for a lunch break and I wasn't overly keen on being in the same room as Pete. Somehow, I got the feeling that it could turn out to be an unpleasant and messy experience. The half-eaten sandwich was evidence of this. Fortunately, it was a nice warm day, so I decided to take my lunch outside and sit on a little seat by a pump house.

Pete thought this was a bit odd, surely a warm, cosy, smelly office was much nicer? I nearly forgot the money, which I put on the desk. Pete insisted that it was fifty-fifty noting that there would no point in trying to find the original owners. Good point!

My first day was steady and enjoyable and Pete left me to my own devices for most of the time. He did a few things which required his skills and experience interspersed with periods of keeping the office chair warm.

Around mid-afternoon, he said that we'd hit the road to call in at another smaller plant before heading for home.

The vehicle was a small commercial van, the rear of which was packed with various tools and spare equipment along with what appeared to be a load of junk. Pete seemed to make no effort to keep the van anything like clean and tidy.

I didn't drive and sharing with Pete was stressful and physically exacting as he drove like a wild thing. The turmoil of the journey made me feel nauseous, that, along with the smell of Pete's grubby overalls nearly caused my lunch to make a second appearance.

Over the ensuing days we settled down into a routine of work. My mentor making the most of my willingness to do whatever was necessary, whilst I relished the fresh air whenever the opportunity arose.

I wondered how Jeff put up with this day in and day out?

Keith and Ron told me that he, (Jeff), was a very easy going and stoical chap, who seemed able to somehow 'absorb' his pugnacious colleague. I really admired Jeff!

I enjoyed being outside and the Gods were kind to me because it only rained on four days during my tenure, even then, I was usually quite happy to put up with it. I'd been given excellent protective clothing, which included waterproof jacket and trousers, along with two pairs of work boots.

On one of these rainy days, I was left with no option but to have lunch with Pete.

He ate noisily and tried to eat his brick sized sandwiches in two bites. I had to look away; it was just too much. Unfortunately, whilst he was trying to digest this mass, he insisted on talking. Semi-digested lumps of cheese sandwich flew everywhere. Multi-tasking wasn't his thing!

I know it sounds like I'm hammering this guy and giving him a hard time, but he was challenging. I cannot pretend otherwise.

It's at this point that I'd like to make one thing clear. It was not a smelly job. True, there was a lingering background odour but it wasn't that invasive – it did not stink! One might have expected vast pools of festering excrement, but this certainly was not the case. It amazed me how "clean" the places were. Well – apart from Pete's little office. There was, however, one rather smelly bit. The sludge or settling tank/pit, which only smelt when it was being emptied and this was done once or twice a week.

A tanker lorry came and sucked the contents out. The bulk of the material was largely dirty water. However, the "bottom bit", where the contents had settled, was thick, gluttonous and slimy. It was also somewhat malodorous.

The tank, sump or whatever its technical designation, was inclined. It was shallow at one end gradually deepening along its length; thus, allowing the suction hose to suck up as much muck as possible. It was a bit like a swimming pool with a shallow and deep end, not that a quick dip was recommended.

However, there was a caveat. The dregs had to be pushed down to the deep end with a kind of rake. Not one with spikes but a hard rubber blade. Someone – had to go down into the abyss and push the remaining slop towards the hose; and that someone, was me. Call me Muggins!

Pete, apparently, had more important things to do! I think the office chair was getting cold?

Despite the nature of the contents of the tank, it didn't really smell *that* bad. However, it looked absolutely vile. If I didn't look down too much, it was okay.

I pushed it all down to the end and the tanker lorry sucked it up. Job done!

Another area requiring a lot of attention was the "trickle beds" or trickling filter. Typically, these were/are circular, between 10 metres and 20 metres across and about 2 metres deep. A circular wall, often of brick, contained a bed of filter media, made up of crushed stones, which in turn rested on a base of under-drains. If you have seen a sewage plant they are quite distinctive and recognizable, with four long, distributor arms going around and around discharging water coming out of evenly spaced nozzles along their length.

These rotor arms required regular cleaning by means of what looked like a very long loo brush.

One took the end cap off and inserted the brush to clear an excessive debris.

However – there was one item of debris which demanded a bit more attention. For some bizarre reason, frogs found these irresistible, which was unfortunate as they tended to get trapped in them. It was not uncommon to see the arms go around with a frog's leg dangling from a nozzle. And – they were a bugger to clear. I only ever rescued one alive. Sadly, it had lost a leg.

For the duration of my tenure, I tended to get on with things, leaving Pete to issues which required his experience and know-how.

We would go from plant to plant as required and, between us, do what needed to be done. Cleaning, clearing, oiling and testing; removing the booty from the channels and filters to share – coinage that is, and ensuring that all the incoming shit never found its way back out; at least not in its raw state.

It is a vital and essential public service. We ALL excrete waste, and, generally speaking – rarely give it a second thought.

Boy – did I feel proud!

Did you know that it was reckoned humans pass over 290 BILLION kgs of poop a year? I can't help but feel some statisticians need to get a life.

Getting back to the poor, much, maligned Pete. I did make the stupid mistake of mentioning Maggie Thatcher one day, although I cannot remember in what context. He went ballistic! His fury knew no bounds and his swearing reached new heights. I counted some 18 Fs and at least 14 Cs. And – we nearly left the road on three occasions. I was stupid enough to mention Mrs T whilst he was driving! What a fucking idiot!!

So - there we have it – a concise and cursory recollection of my time at the sewage plants.
Did I enjoy it?
Yes – I did really. Ironically, it was a good healthy job and Pete was an extraordinary man. I'm not being sarcastic – he was powerful and uncompromising, yet possessed – at times, the milk human

kindness. That, in my book, is a fine and laudable quality.

In many ways, I grew quite fond of him; he was so "human". I think – looking back – he enriched my life. Yes! Now there's a fucking surprise. And – working with shit certainly broadened my outlook.

The Last Post

This tale is a bit out of sync because it's something I did whilst waiting to **go back** into nursing. The new ward – in a very old building; was far from ready. I wasn't too sure what I was going to do with myself, when this cropped up. A fixed term contract with Royal Rail at the local Post Office, which had a little sorting office in a long, narrow outbuilding out the back.

Not rocket science and very easy to pick up. A few days on-the-job training and I was off! Of course, I had to conform to the very strict Royal Mail code of practice and conduct, the main one being to sign up to a strict code of confidentiality.

My duty involved delivering post around the centre of the little rural town where we lived.

It encompassed a mix of commercial and residential deliveries.

My starting time was 5.30am, which meant leaving home at 5.10 to make the 15/20-minute walk to the sorting office.

The first task each morning was to sort out the sacks of mail which were brought in from the main delivery centre, some 4 miles away. These were then sorted into "rounds". Each round was then taken by the person who did that duty to be re-sorted into address order. The aim was to ensure a logical delivery route. I hope that is clear?

I was joining a team of 8 other posties. And what an interesting group they were. I couldn't resist evaluating them.

The guy working next to me was an affable and loquacious cockney; at least, he sounded like a cockney. I thought I could hear Bow Bells? He worked fast and talked fast. I soon gathered he had a wife and three children. His one aim was to sort his mail and get out on the road. His round was out 'in the sticks' delivering to a few of the outlying villages and farms.

Next down was a jovial chap in his mid to late 40s, who appeared to be to be something of a mainstay. He came across as a steady pair of hands; always cheery and agreeable, little or nothing affected his easy-going nature. He just got on with the job. He was the one the others turned to with any queries or problems.

Following him was a guy, roughly the same age, who, by contrast, was quite edgy and anxious. Fretful and restive, he sighed a lot! Never-the-less, he was always genial and companionable.

Sitting next to him at the end of the row was a woman in her mid to late 50s who was a 'bit of a character'. She was blunt, forthright, loud and free with her opinions, which she expressed in no uncertain terms. Frequently challenging and confrontational; she also had *very* bad teeth!

Across from her worked a rather timid and quiet lady, who said very little and kept herself to herself. She was friendly enough and always polite, but reserved.

Up from her was a lovely lady, who came across as motherly and warm. She was a good friend of "Bellicose Lady" but very different in her attitude and demeanour. She was chief tea maker and therefore much valued and appreciated.

Which left the two posties who were stationed behind me. They were, so I was quickly informed, "in a relationship", and it soon became very apparent that they were not the most popular people in the room. Bellicose Lady made it clear that she didn't like them. And if she didn't like you, you knew it!

Just to be clear, it was a heterosexual relationship.

From my perspective, they were friendly enough and perfectly civil. Quite frankly, I just wanted to get on and leave well alone. I was there as a Temp and had no desire to get involved in the dynamics, or wrapped up in any internal politics.

Finally, there was the postmaster. A blunt and taciturn man, who was a stickler for propriety. He would not tolerate any nonsense or malpractice. We got on well enough and were little more than ships in the night anyway. Many was the time Bellicose Lady tested his patience and he found the "lovebirds" (the relationship pair), something of a trial. He did not hide his disapproval and vociferously denounced the association.

We were only all together for an hour or so each morning and there was rarely anyone in the office when I returned at the end of my duty. If I met up with anybody, it was usually timid, quiet lady and we'd just smile and exchange the odd nicety and that was that.

So – all sorted and bagged up, I hit the streets to deliver the mail.

The first part of my circuit was close to the office in and around the town centre. The addresses were largely commercial – small shops and offices, with a few houses and flats here and there. It didn't take too long depending on the volume of post; my bag rarely bulged with mail, unless there happened to be several large parcels, packets or document envelopes.

Some items had to held back because many of the shops etc. didn't open until 9am. I soon learnt that it was better leaving any large items at the office, so I could go back later and not have to carry it all around with me.

Being a small town – perhaps more of a large village; it was a friendly place which made the job so much easier and a lot more enjoyable. There were a few crusty buggers who moaned if I was a little late on my return visits, but most were patient and polite.

One of the biggest whingers was a small accountancy group, who often received recorded mail, which, of course, required a signature and had to be done on a second visit.

"How can we be expected to get on with our days work if the post is late? We need reliability and a prompt service!" (Blah, blah, blah!)

I gave up trying to explain and just let the grumbles drift in one ear and quickly out of the other.

One of the friendliest places was a small set of offices owned by a company of solicitors, just above a newsagents. I was always treated well there and took a real shine to the receptionist – a lovely and very attractive lady, who I guessed to be in her early 40s. I had a real soft spot for her and, seeing her warm open smile often made my day.

One day, I had to make a return visit for a special delivery. She was over the moon, it was, apparently, very important and for my troubles, I received a "thank you" kiss! I nearly caught fire!

What would my wife say?

I'll tell you. She laughed and teased me relentlessly about it. They knew one another! Ah – the duplicity of women!!

I also called into a lovely little bakery, wherein I was usually treated to a donut or scone, and a delicatessen where I took a small sample of the "Cheese of the Day". Yes – I know we were not supposed to accept gratuities, but where was the harm for goodness sake?

The second part of my round was in a small residential area of some 150 houses. This was usually straightforward domestic mail delivery.

Many of the homes were council houses and made provision for those of – how can I put it – lesser means. I hope that doesn't sound demeaning or denigrating? My background was soundly working class, having been brought up on a shabby council estate which had an awful reputation. It was the sort of place where if a mother left her baby outside in its pram; not only might the pram get nicked, the baby could disappear as well. Sadly – my visits to some of the letterboxes were not always welcome because, all to commonly, many envelopes had "Final Demand" written across the top. I'd certainly received a few of those over the years, and, yes – they did not make for happy reading. It became a bit prickly and awkward when these were sent recorded delivery; some were reluctant to sign for them, thereby acknowledging receipt and increasing the fear that the bailiffs might be on their way. I found this quite challenging at times; I was the harbinger of bad news and potential trouble.

On the other side of the coin, I also delivered Birthday and Christmas cards.

I have a shameful admission to make here. I was a very bad man; a very bad man indeed. On birthdays, one often watched out eagerly for the postman, who, all being well, would deliver lots of cards and presents. His/her bag possibly heaving with goodies; although that was never really the case.

Anyway – one could often see eager little faces at the window, full of anticipation.

On one such occasion, I spotted the eager little face and walked straight by. The effect was dramatic as I heard a heart-breaking howl.

Although I was only trying to be playful, I felt like pond-scum; a real low-life.

I quickly returned to be greeted by an anxious looking mother and a greatly relieved child, with a tear-streaked face. Mercifully, I sometimes carried a bar of chocolate in my bag and was able to add an extra gift to the collection.

I repeat. I felt (and deserved to feel) – deeply ashamed.

The post often contained slightly unusual items, like smoked salmon. This was always an essential "special delivery". It had to be delivered quickly and before 12 noon. It was vacuum packed and well-sealed, but it couldn't hang around.

I found myself delivering this on two separate occasions. The first was trouble free, whilst the second was problematic; the recipient refused it saying it was "off".

Nothing I could do or say would change the customers mind, so I had to take it back to the office.

The postmaster was less than happy but contacted the supplier. He was told write a report and get a statement from me, then have it for himself as sending it back would have been pointless.

The customer would NOT get a refund.

I was a bit peeved because, he was usually a fair man but on this occasion he was not inclined to share this unexpected bonus. Git!!!

One of the most common tales regarding post-persons is that of encounters with dogs. Well, I soon discovered that these were not tall tales as I became acquainted with a black dog who I christened Cujo. He – for it was definitely a male – was a calculating and cunning little shit who delighted in hounding me. Pun intended!

He would lurk and keep a low profile until I was in firing range. He got one bite in and made several other attempts before I got hold of a folding walking stick, which I kept in my bag. This – thank goodness – was deterrent enough.

One day, I saw this canine nemesis out for a walk with its owner. They walked towards me and the darn mutt started to wag its tail. I obviously looked a bit apprehensive, so the owner made it clear that he "was a good dog and very friendly, so I needn't worry."

Yeah – right. Mangy mutt was just playing nicely for its owner.

I really enjoyed this career escape; on a warm, sunny, clear day – it was a delight. Conversely, when it was cold and wet, the appeal wore off. However, the Royal Mail provided excellent and effective outdoor wear. Ice and/or snow, made for hard going with heavy mail bags, but this was eased by the provision of snow grips which were strapped to our shoes, although I only ever used these once as they were a bit awkward.

Another perk, of sorts, was the hours. We were paid for our contract hours. Mine were 5.30 – 10.30am, and yet many was the time I was all done by 9.00am. Very nice!

Of course, at 'heavy' times I usually worked up to my time, and occasionally beyond, for which I was paid extra.

I did this for just under a year, after which, I returned to nursing and a little hospital which turned out to be the best I ever worked in.

But understand this – these were the days before mass emails, or any emails. There was no online shopping; no Amazon. Post was real – letters, bills, real information. How things have changed.

One final thing.

Apart from that bloody dog, I never met with any customer aggression. A few grumbles, but nothing excessive. Apart from one guy who hated leaflets going through his letterbox.

As with today, the Royal Mail, by arrangement, agreed to deliver product advertisement leaflets. This was a way in which the posties could earn a little bit extra. Like today, they were not that popular.

The man in question was extremely anti and took issue with me.

"Oi! Stop putting these fucking things through my door. I don't want them and didn't ask for them, so stop dumping this shit on my doormat."

We were supposed to deliver the leaflets to *every* address, without exception! However, after careful and due consideration, and as an act of self-preservation, I never put anymore through his letterbox.

And here, good people, endeth the "Postie Days"!

Rest In Peace

In so many ways, this was the highlight of my venture into the "outside world".
I knew it was time to think about settling down job wise so I thought I would have one last fling.
Scouring the situations vacant in the local snooze-paper, something caught my eye.
Temporary position available at local crematorium – or words to that effect. Part-time 5 days a week. Ideal candidate needs to be calm, composed and sympathetic. Working in challenging environment the person must be respectful and considerate at all times. Good, established people skills are essential.
Anyway – it went something like that.
"*Yes. That's me,*" I thought. Or could be.

The crematorium was about 2 or 3 miles away and on the main bus route. It would then leave a short 15 minute walk from the bus stop to the facility.

I applied and got the job!

The first thing I had to do was get down to Marks and Spencer's with a chitty, to buy a suit – dark grey, with light pin stripes. This was to be my uniform.

As for my place of work. The crematorium building, although some years old was of a modern, and, some might say, radical design. Fundamentally, it was a giant sloping roof!

There were 5 other people making up the team. A manager, an assistant manager and an administrative assistant.

Out in the chapel and crematorium itself, a man about my age and – to my great surprise – a young lady, covered chapel and cremation duties.

These were the two people who I would be working most closely with.

The young lady seemed no more than a girl, although she was 20 years old; and, I must add, very capable.

It's not that age mattered; far from it. I suppose it was just a perception? "What was a young girl doing working in a place like this – burning bodies?"

My job was to cover chapel duties working over the extended lunchtime period.

I wasn't at all sure how I'd deal with people going in at gas mark 10, but they were, of course, dead; and, one assumed, had elected to be cremated? By that time, it was too late anyway.

I didn't honestly think it would bother me and it didn't. I was no stranger to death, having worked in dementia care for so long. This was just the "last bit".

For the sake of easy identification, and as there were only five of them, I'll give my cohorts names. The manager – Mark, the assistant manager – Steve, the administrative assistant – Gail and my two closest colleagues – Nigel and Carol. They were trained cremators, and needed to be; as it was stringently regulated and strictly controlled.

I soon realized how meaningful and special the job was.

It was the final curtain call and a privilege to be a part of this last act.

The little things mattered. Making sure the chapel was ready and prepared, with everything as it should be. Ensuring the hymn and prayer books in place and to hand; that orders of service were placed as requested.

At such a stressful time, it was rewarding to see it running smoothly and flawlessly.

One of the key duties was housekeeping – vacuuming, dusting and polishing; not forgetting keeping the toilets pristine!

One of the things I looked forward to was the choice of music, which could be extremely varied. Old standards, favourite classical works; Country and Western was very popular. There was never any shortage of diversity. Even Led Zeppelin made a showing on one occasion.

One song which really got on my nerves because it was in vogue at the time and seen as rather 'celestial' was – "I Believe I Can Fly" by R. Kelly.

One service requested a song from the 1920s – "The Laughing Policeman" by

Charles Jolly, or Penrose as he was also known. It certainly made for a cheerful service, as did "The Ying-Tong Song" by The Goons!

Services could be very individual, and choices varied and diverse. Religious and Non-Religious, Humanist, Multi-cultural and all manner of themes reflecting faith and/or beliefs.

Every once in awhile, there would be what was known as a "non-service"; wherein there was no congregation and nobody leading. These were sad, poignant affairs so we made something of it by making up a small congregation, with a few simple words and some music at committal.

There was one, however, which stood out for the wrong reasons.

A hearse arrived at the facility with a coffin in the back. Well, no surprise there; they rarely

arrived empty. There were no flowers; and –
the weather had been very hot!

The undertakers were unknown to us and
had travelled some 20 odd miles to deliver
the "customer". The odd thing was that they
seemed in an awful rush.

Obviously, we were expecting the service
and were prepared to do our thing; all
services were pre-booked. Can you imagine
turning up with a body unannounced in the
hope that it could be popped in the oven on
the off-chance?

Anyway – I digress. These chaps were in a
hurry and their haste was initially rather
puzzling as they literally jogged in
shouldering the coffin; dropped it on the
catafalque and legged it.

When we went out to look our noses soon
gave the game away. There was a
noticeable and sickly aroma in the air. It was

very unpleasant, and we were very angry.
This poor souls' body had obviously not
been properly prepared.

Because of this we said a few words and
whisked it out into the cremation room, tout
suite!!

No life is meaningless, and whether there
are 200 mourners or 2 – or none; a life has
ended, a life, which, (hopefully), had been
lived. Every life leaves a mark and those little
bespoke services certainly left a mark on
me.

Knowing that I worked at a crematorium
appeared to fascinate and intrigue some
people and the same questions often arose.
Did they burn the right body and were the
ashes those of *that* person?

Yes! Absolutely! As I have stated previously
– it all had strict protocols and procedures.

The other question was – did they stack the bodies up and burn them altogether?

I refer the honourable gentleman to my previous answer.

The cremators could only take ONE coffin and it was the right coffin. Cremation usually took place within minutes of the service ending. Occasionally, there was a short wait during busy periods, but bodies were never 'stored'.

The ashes were carefully collected and there was no room for confusion. Mrs Jones went in and what remained of Mrs Jones came out.

However, cremation was rarely complete. The ashes still contained some solid material. These were put into a cremulator, which was a bit like a tumble dryer but full of large metal balls. The remains were put into this machine to be ground down to ash.

Next to the cremulator was a large bin; this contained artificial joints, mostly hip. I was never quite sure what happened to these. One of the greatest fears was the remote possibility that a pacemaker had been left inside a body. This could be quite dangerous as they would explode in the cremator. Double checks were made prior to any cremation to ensure that these had been removed. Of course, this happened elsewhere.

My "station" as a Service Attendant was a little room adjacent to the chapel opposite the catafalque, or bier. It had a one way window – I could see out, but I could not be seen. This meant that that the service could be closely followed. It allowed the service leader to pass discrete signs and gestures to me – when to start the music of draw the curtains, which were electrically operated.

Some service leaders preferred to do this themselves.

Most – I'd say 98% - services were carried off with dignity, decorum and respect. However, one or two failed to achieve this. It was rare, but unpleasant and abhorrent. One such debacle involved a family of two halves. The deceased had remarried and became the head of two separate families. Sadly – there appeared to be little unity and, from the outset, the atmosphere was tense. The "first family" taking to one side of the chapel and the "second family" sitting on the other.

The trigger came about when one of his daughters from the left side of the chapel moved forward to touch the coffin as it was placed on the catafalque. This prompted a sudden and brusque response from another

daughter, from the right side. She accused
the other of hypocrisy and posturing.
Matters got out of hand very quickly as
tempers flared. It became abusive and
aggressive. Almost a brawl.
The service was stopped by the conducting
vicar and lead undertaker.
It was a disgraceful display.
After a brief lull, the service resumed –
minus the two women. The service had to be
'edited' as time was running short.
Services were often limited by available time
and back-to-back services were quite
common.
Another upset came about at the funeral of a
former rugby coach when two of the
congregation turned up very drunk. There
was no doubting their level of inebriation;
they could barely stand. From the outset,
they were very noisy and disruptive.

They were spoken to by the undertaker, who politely asked them to settle down or leave. They became very abusive. Mark and Steve were called but the men would not listen; becoming even more belligerent. As a result, the police were called. In the meantime, two other attendees, who knew them, managed to get them out of the chapel. As a consequence of this the service had to be considerably shortened because another was following close behind. I felt so sorry for the rest of the congregation.

Another little duty which occasionally came my way was to bury ashes out in the lovely grounds.

The area was marked off into defined areas were the ashes were interred. This was to enable visits to a particular location, should people wish to do so. It wasn't an exact science but usually within a few inches.

Using an auger to bore a hole 6 inches in diameter, you first made a cut about an inch deep, this forms the cap which acts as a seal when you'd finished. You then drilled down a good 18 inches and cleared the hole. The ashes were tipped into the hole, topped up with spoil then sealed off with the cap. All the locations were then recorded for identification purposes.

It was not common but occasionally we received requests to remove the ashes for relocation.

It always seemed a bit of a shame, because having been in the ground, they became bonded with the soil, and, unsurprisingly, they deteriorated. It was an unusual request, but one which had to be honoured.

Another little job was clearing all the old decaying flowers. These were collected up and put into a skip, which filled up very quickly. The flowers looked so beautiful for a day or two but wilted very quickly. I always thought that this was such a shame.

I enjoyed being out in the grounds – they were lovely, so I made the most of it.

For the sake of clarity; I didn't wear my suit for this, I had a warehouse coat and boots for these tasks.

I have referred to services but have avoided specifics. I was often asked if it bothered me?

No – it didn't. It was obviously emotional and affecting, but there was an inevitability about it. For the most part – the services were for those who, on the face of it, had lived something akin to a "full life".

However – I *did* find the funerals of babies and children very challenging. I only ever attended a few, but that was more than enough.

I grew fond of this job; it created a unique awareness of life, odd as that may sound. I'd witnessed death so many times, but it didn't end there.

The experiences I had here were invaluable. It never made me feel miserable or maudlin; indeed, I now appreciated life more than ever.

I never did anything quite like this again. How could I?

In retrospect, it became something of a turning point and I rather liked the direction it pointed me in.

When I left I was allowed to keep my suit, which I still wear on rare occasions.

I'd like to add one last thing regarding coffins.

To be honest, I've become quite cynical about these boxes, which we end up in. They *looked* grand and ornate. Well – it soon became apparent that this was an illusion. Seen close up, many were cheap and tacky with fragile plastic fittings and "mock" wood.

At the end of the day, they were going to get burnt or dropped in a dark, dank hole. All I'm saying is that appearances can be deceptive!

I lied – there is another "last thing". Overwhelmed by ghoulish curiosity, I did, eventually, look at a body burning.

All the cremators had observation glasses so the process could be monitored. I looked. In fact I looked on several occasions, and, in all honesty – it didn't have much of an impact. It no longer registered as a person. It was almost a case of – "that's that!"

And – let's face it. It was!

Back Home

This is a last-minute addition wherein I decided to bring things to a close, in a concise but clear way. At least, that is the intention.

After my tour around the situations vacant and journey around Job-land, I returned to the wards, working in a small dementia care unit housed in a long, narrow wooden hut. It would not have looked out of place in any POW camp. I could almost hear "Tenko!" Having said this, don't get the wrong impression, despite the confinements of what could be done with such a building, it was well fitted out and more than adequate. It was fit for purpose, despite being well past its sell-by date.

The patients – as they were called then – were those living with dementia.

It was a wonderful place to work and I was very happy there; the team were a real joy to work with.

To my complete and utter amazement, I knew the manager who had trained a few groups ahead of me at my training hospitals. She had not been present at my interview but had been happy to endorse my appointment. Ah, the "old boys" network! I've described what it is like to work in such area in "You Don't Have To Be Mad", so I'll not regurgitate all that that.

Fundamentally, the good souls needed a lot of support, most being completely dependent on nursing care.

One might have been tempted to take the view that: "the lights were on, but no one was in".

Wrong – very wrong!

For example.

One morning, we were all sat enjoying a bit of a tea-break; by all, I mean patients as well; that is those who were not bedridden. It was a hot day and the huts were sweltering, so we decided to open a few more windows.

Sat nearby, at a table, was a lady who rarely said much, and appeared not to notice things. To our utter amazement, she piped up said with absolute clarity – "Ouvrez la fenêtre." (Open the window).

We discovered later from a relative that she'd once lived in France. The same relative also said there was a rumour that she had been a SOE (Special Operations Executive), operative; however, this could not be verified.

In similar circumstances; one of the nursing auxiliaries, who was sitting at a table knitting; (she was making something for one of the patients), and did a bit here and there when she could; which because of the workload wasn't very often.

She was called away and left the knitting on the table. It was picked up by another female patient, who rarely engaged with anyone or anything. She immediately carried on with the knitting, and it was perfect. She did say that she thought the stitching was a bit lose!

For me, personally, this was so developmental. I'd never been a confident nurse and tended to doubt myself. I lacked professional courage and struggled to generate a positive image. This was not good and that's putting it mildly. As a qualified, and experienced nurse I *had* to up my game. I needed to be much more courageous and bolder.

Working here reinvigorated me and gave a vital pick-me-up; an essential battery charge. In a very short time, the worm turned. Supported and inspired by a great team, I found something of the lion in the lamb.

I was the only male member of staff and reliving this reminds of how things have changed; in particular, behaviour at work – how we interacted and behaved with each other.

In today's, (2018) hypersensitive environment, wherein a firm line is taken on anything remotely resembling abuse in the workplace, our behaviour **then** might well have caused unrestrained outrage. There would be disciplinary action and general uproar.

We teased each other, pinched bottoms and exchanged playful ribaldry. On hot days, when the place was like an oven, the "girls" would loosen their uniform tops, exposing more flesh than normal. It was inoffensive and never misconstrued or misinterpreted. There were boundaries and our mutual respect and team spirit defined those boundaries. That would *not* stand today!!

I'm convinced that my journey around other jobs helped immensely, I felt worldlier, more aware and enlightened.
I'd found the real nurse in me, some 20 years or so after I qualified.
As much as I loved the unit and the wonderful people, it all started to feel regressive; I'd been there for over 3 years and felt it was time to move on.
The decision to leave was, in part, affected by a series of unforeseen events; nothing at all serious, just an opportunity to look through another door.

I stayed in healthcare moving to another area to work in Day and Community Care within the mental healthcare service.

I returned to the locality where I did my training. Both hospitals had closed and were partially demolished, making way for state of the art pokey apartments.

This was quite fresh and revitalizing.

For all my previous experience in mental health it represented quite a shift because nearly everything I'd done was in-patient care.

The focus was on supporting those who lived at home or in the community, enabling them to remain that way; empowering them, helping them cope with life in the community. At least that was the spin!

Initially – I was based in a Day Centre which acted as a social hub. Offering a wide range of carefully planned activities for those who wished to take part, along with interactive discussion sessions.

However, if an individual just wanted company, tea and lunch; that was fine. It was an open door.

The Centre had a mini-bus which was put to good use taking "service users" (patients) on day-trip outings.

However – I find it hard not to appear cynical. I'd always been sceptical about the 'wonders' of care in the community, having seen little evidence that it was actually working.

This attitude hardened here because several of the attendees were patients I knew from my training days. They did not appear to have made much headway and attended the Day Centre "under instruction"; often unwillingly.

They lived in community micro-units, in relative isolation. All the bullshit hyperbole just evaporated.

I had a few years at the Centre, before moving on the work in a community group "home", accommodating 6 people who lived with enduring mental health issues. Most had been in hospital for many years. One man had been in Broadmoor (the high security hospital), for some years. And - yet again, there were old faces, from my formative years, who just looked – older!

To be honest, and it pains me to say this; it was little more than a mini hospital. These people lived in a community setting, but they were not involved in it. They were not integrating in any way, shape or form. For all the good intentions they still lived fairly closeted lives.

But – the home was closing down; the NHS could no longer sustain it. As a result, the tenants were to be moved from the place in which they felt safe and relatively secure into private supported accommodation. It was **extremely** stressful and traumatic for them. They moved out gradually over a period of a few weeks, until one remained, the Broadmoor guy, who was as gentle as a lamb. And, my very last shift involved me staying with him for the night. Despite his obviously unease and apprehension, he slept through the night with me "on guard". It was incredibly boring. As a result, I slept for several hours, unable to keep my eyes open.

That was nearly the end of my NHS career. However – things took a slightly odd turn when I was offered a non-nursing post in the local general hospital.

My job was to ensure that some of the medical equipment used on the wards, was fit for purpose and readily available when required.

Fundamentally – it involved going around the hospital collecting used equipment and taking it back to be thoroughly cleaned and checked ready for reuse. It involved a *lot* of walking – it is a big hospital!

This was a good, steady job to go out on and helped bolster my pension a little as an added bonus.

A few years later – I retired.

Now – I will test you.

Did you note the "sub-title" of this little tome?

– "(And breaking a leg)"

There is a reason for this.

Two weeks after leaving my job; I broke my leg. The first serious injury I had ever sustained. I was in plaster for 6 weeks.

There is a caveat to this, and, to my mind, a very important one.

For three weeks I was virtually immobile. There wasn't a lot I could do, which I found ***extremely*** frustrating.

To coincide with this lay-up, the November weather turned cold, gloomy and dismal. In no time at all, my mood started to go the same way; it dropped like a stone. I was on my own for up to 10 hours a day and confined.

Feelings and thoughts, the like of which I'd never encountered, overwhelmed me. Like most people, I'd had "bad days" and "downs", but this was more intense and insidious. It was like a thick, dark, shadowy cloak.

I accepted that it was reactionary and not endogenous, but it was suffocating, and – very frightening.

For a few weeks I battled this trying to rationalize and escape it.

Liberation came gradually as I became more active, day-on-day.

On my first real outing – a (very) gentle walk over to a nearby local park; I cried. I could not stop myself.

The place I had been to shook me to the core. But what insights it gave me. After all my years working in mental health; this was a game changer. I felt true and overwhelming empathy.

Of course, deep, clinical endogenous depression is utterly debilitating; mercifully, I hadn't gone down that road. But I do believe I got a flavour of it, and it was very unpleasant.

And there ended my 48-year work history.

Thank you for sharing these memories with me. I hope you found something of interest. I hope you didn't get too bored?

Despite the fact that this was unplanned, I am glad that I was 'encouraged' to put it all together.

Now, I really do think that enough is enough and have no desire to flog the poor horse anymore. There are limits and I *really* do need to move on.

Looking back, I've had a good time; not that I intend that to sound "final". It isn't the end; just a chapter closing.

With sincere and best wishes.

Gordon Tozer - November 2018.

31503207R00049

Printed in Poland
by Amazon Fulfillment
Poland Sp. z o.o., Wrocław